ALLAN MORRISON is a prolific auth
Ma Chips, Ah've Drapped the Wea
Last Tram tae Auchenshuggle! and *Kerryoans up the Cly...*
pearances include *The One Show* and *The Fred MacAulay Show*. He is involved in charity work and after-dinner speaking, and is a member of his local Rotary club. Allan enjoys hill-walking, sport and travel. He and his wife live in the West of Scotland and he is the proud grandfather of four grandchildren.

'Dinna Fash Yersel, Scotland!'

Scottish Grannies' Sayings for Challenging Times

ALLAN MORRISON
Illustrations by
BOB DEWAR

Luath Press Limited

EDINBURGH

www.luath.co.uk

First published 2022

ISBN: 978-1-80425-048-8

The paper used in this book is recyclable. It is made
from low chlorine pulps produced in a low energy,
low emission manner from renewable forests.

Printed and bound by
Robertson Printers, Forfar

Typeset in Freight Text Pro and Brando Sans by
Main Point Books, Edinburgh

Contents

Introduction

THE WORLD IS going through a difficult time with many worrying challenges in all aspects of life.

However, grannies can be an oasis of calm with their thoughtful observations, wisdom and wise warnings. You see, grannies are positive and have the mental strength to deal with situations. They have a wealth of knowledge and experience. No messing around with them. They go directly to the nub of the problem and have much to offer. It is true that when the going gets tough the tough get going.

Scottish sayings are usually short, quirky and directly address situations we all encounter in life. In essence, a catch phrase with purpose. Some of the sayings in this book are contemporary but most are older. They will hopefully be helpful as they provide reassurance to those who seek it, and make you smile with their direct humour. The key element is they are relevant to the difficult times we live in, with common sense being the basis to them all.

Cost of Living

'Dinnae stretch yer erm oot further than yer sleeve.'

Do not spend what you can't afford.

'Getting up's mair important than fallin' doon.'

Keep going regardless of your situation.

'Ye cannae steal a coo fae a man who has nane.'

Some people have no money and therefore cannot pay at present.

'If ye cannae afford tae go, dinnae go!'

Don't overstretch your finances.

'Nae debt is good fur yer health.'

Worry about money owed can be a great burden on you.

'Even efter a bad harvest ye must sow.'

Even if you are having a difficult time, you should plan ahead to hopefully much better times.

'Close they windaes. Yer heatin' the hale o' Scotland.'

Don't waste money.

'Don't jist dae nothing; dae something aboot it!'

Don't just wallow in despair; try and fix it.

'Ye cannae tak pennies oot an empty puggy.'

So, try and do something to refill your purse.

'Castles fall but wise words stay.'

Common sense will hopefully prevail.

'Cut yer coat tae suit yer pattern.'

Only spend what you can truly afford.

'Let's like whit we can get.'

Since we cannot always get what we like.

'He who disnae open his eyes when he buys must still open his wallet when he pays.'

Watch what you are getting into.

'Worry is like an auld rockin' chair. It gies ye somethin' tae dae but disnae get you ony where.'

Be upfront with your problems and fix them.

'Getting free o' debt is springtime.'

Your winter is over and better times are ahead.

'The Money Man's deid!'

Sorry. We cannot continue with this present situation. Try another solution.

'Dinnae waste a penny candle huntin' fur a bawbee.'

Get your financial priorities right.

'Dinnae eat the calf in the coo's womb.'

Don't spend money you don't yet have.

'Anything is better than a slap on the dial wi' a wet haddie.'

Even a small amount of extra money is most welcome.

'Experience teaches fools, an' fools willna learn nae ither way.'

Some people only learn through bitter experience.

'There is aye someone wull tell ye times are tough. But jist ye keep going!'

Remain positive, even if other people are panicking.

'The only thing ye can dae on a shoestring is trip.'

You need to be careful if you have limited funds.

'Dinnae gae intae worry an' despair. They're a right pair o' rogues.'

Don't get downhearted.

'If ye dinna see the bottom then dinna wade.'

If you cannot see a successful conclusion, then don't do it.

He's a fool who asks ower muckle, an' a bigger fool that pays.'

Selling something at an inflated price is not good practice, and anyone who pays the price is unwise.

'Hunger wid break through stane wa's.'

Hunger can drive people to desperation.

'Ye cannae sell the cow an' sup the milk.'

Watch what you are doing. Think on the implications of your actions.

'Rainbows come oot o' rain drops.'

Sometimes difficulties prove to have been of an unlikely benefit in the long run.

'Fight yer way through the bad days tae get tae the good days.'

Keep going and things may eventually turn out well.

'Listen. Ah wis brought up in Poverty Hall, so aw ye can dae is pull in yer purse strings.'

Be very careful with the little you have.

'Don't jist sit there an' mope or ye'll end up wi' a face like a wet Sunday.'

Feeling sorry for yourself doesn't resolve the problem.

'Live modestly and keep Mister and Mrs Bills away fae yer door.'

Don't be over extravagant.

'Cost o' living only stops at the cemetery.'

The cost of living is always there during our lives.

'Santa Claus didnae bring a parcel o' worry tae ye. Ye brought it yersel.'

Your own actions cause the problems.

'Nae matter how far ye have travelled in the wrong direction, you can always turn roon.'

At some point you can change and sort yourself out.

'Thanks disnae pay the fiddler.'

You need money to pay your bills.

'Askin' fur help is no' a sign o' weakness.'

There is no shame in requiring assistance.

'If ye lose it in the fire ye'll find it in the ashes.'

Eventually you will be able to recover.

'If ye dinna feed the cat ye'll feed the mice.'

Do it now or the situation may get worse.

'If the cost o' livin' goes up much mair the chance o' livin' the high life wull come doon.'

Just live according to your means.

'There are three sides tae aw things.'

There is usually more than one solution to a problem.

'Dinnae burn doon the barn tae get rid o' the mice.'

Don't take extreme measures. Take a measured approach to your problems.

'A troot in the pan is better than a salmon in the Tay.'

Better to have a little than something you may never have.

'A pun o' care winna pay an ounce o' debt.'

You require action to address problems.

'Even oak trees struggle in a guid blaw.'

Everyone can have problems from time to time.

'Naethin' is got wi' delay but dirt an' lang nails.'

It does not pay to procrastinate.

'Hang a thief when he's young, an' he'll no' steal when he's auld.'

Fix problems as quickly as you can.

'The langest day wull hae an end.'

Even major problems can be resolved in time.

'Ye cannae buy peace o' mind in the shops.'

You need to sort out your situation yourself.

'When stress sleeps, dinnae wake it.'

Don't go over past problems which no longer exist.

'The pain ye huv aboot money noo is like the strength ye wull feel when ye fix it.'

Once you sort out your money worries it will bring a wonderful feeling of relief when all is well.

'If ye don't struggle tae get there ye'll never get there.'

It may be difficult but you need to persevere.

'A slow fire maks sweet meat.'

Take your time and get it right.

'Dinnae be a twa-legged creature wae a goose's heid an' a hen's heart.'

You must not be afraid to address your problems.

"Tis folly tae live poor an' die rich.'

If you have funds then use them wisely and enjoy life.

'Sometimes forget the cost o' livin' an' jist enjoy the livin' bit.'

You need to stop being worried about the cost of living and have fun.

'Strength o' mind defeats a' things.'

Determination can overcome most situations.

Money

'Every penny's a prisoner.'

Don't be careless with the little you have.

'Dinna sail oot further than ye can row back.'

Know your limitations.

'You that hae but wan e'e maun tend it weel.'

If you have limited assets then be careful with them.

'He that hae twa hoards wull get a third.'

Money creates even more money.

'Mony a mickle maks a muckle.'

Money saved can grow to a fair amount.

'Jump o'er rivers at the burn.'

Address your problems before they become bigger.

'Money disnae buy happiness but being skint buys naethin'.'

We all need some money.

'Earn afore spend.'

Don't put yourself into debt.

'The wife wha kept her supper fur her breakfast wull die.'

Use your funds wisely.

'Time aye beats money. Ye might get more money but never time.'

Watch. You are not here forever.

'Oot on the branch the fruit can be gey ripe.'

Better interest rates and investment require higher risk.

'Dinny jist watch the hole in yer pocket: sew it up.'

Don't be careless with your money.

'Many have o'er much, but nane enough.'

Nobody is truly satisfied with what they have.

'Double check afore ye cut.'

Stop and consider before you make important decisions.

'Some thieves are jist honest men wi' temptation.'

Don't put temptation in the road of anyone.

'The deil's aye guid tae his ain kin.'

People tend to be friendly with others of the same ilk.

'A wolf may lose his teeth but no' his nature.'

Watch out. People do not really change.

'Money should be yer servant, no' yer maister.'

Stay in control of your finances.

'Dinnae pour water on a drooned moose.'

Don't do something that is unnecessary.

'Chase twa blackbirds an' catch nane.'

Be content with what is within your grasp.

'Alexander Graham Bell might've invented it, but he didnae know the rogues that wid use it.'

Be careful when answering phone calls.

'He disnae ken the pleasures o' plenty, wha never felt the pains o' penury.'

If you have had very little, then you appreciate it when you manage to improve things.

'Instead o' crying ower spilt milk go an' buy a coo.'

Address the source of your money problems.

'To the crooked show yersel wise.'

If you suspect someone then be on your guard.

'Invest in yer education; it pays best interest.'

Keep educating and improving yourself.

'Dae ye think Carnegie wis yer uncle?'

You don't have a rich relative so be careful with your spending.

'Wi' nae money ye've nae arrows fur yer bow.'

Your spending is limited.

'Sometimes it's a sair fecht fur half a loaf.'

Is it really worthwhile taking this action?

'Mair than enough is ower muckle.'

Better to be content with what you have.

'Guid steel is worth a penny.'

You have to pay for real quality.

'Any mair snazzle aff you an' ye'll no' be in the hat this week.'

Some people cannot pay all of their bills and so select only one at a time to pay.

'Ah hope aw they hackers die o' a hackin' cough!'

I just hope these fraudsters all come to a bad end.

'He that wad thrive must rise by five, he that has thriven may lie till seven.'

Only if you are already comfortably off can you laze around.

'Nae sweat, nae sweet.'

Good things only come from hard work.

'Worry wilna get ye even a wee roon penny.'

Get on and get busy.

'Jist because it isnae happenin' fur you right noo disnae mean it wull never happen.'

Some things take a while to yield benefit.

'Ye cannae beat that wee fella, "Disnae Gie In".'

It is very difficult to win over someone who refuses to give up.

'Money in the bank is like ridin' a bike. Ye've got tae watch yer balance.'

Always keep up to date with your financial situation.

'They're no' the happiest that hae the maist gear.'

Possessions don't necessarily bring happiness.

'Loosers mak excuses an' winners mak money.'

Aim to be a winner.

'Hae a rich life regardless o' yer siller.'

Enjoy your life even if you are not well off.

'Even in a fallen nest ye may find a whole egg.'

Surely you have something left of value?

'Keep the ba' aff the slates.'

Don't let your debt get beyond your reach.

'Ye canny buy time wi' siller.'

Money can buy most things but not time.

'Better tae say, "here it is" than "here it wis".'

Money to hand is better than money gone.

'It's better ye ken how mony beans mak five.'

Look carefully after your own interests.

'Dinnae eat cake tae save breid.'

Be sensible at all times with your resources.

Being Careful

'Ye could gang faur an fare waur.'

You are better off with where you are at present.

'Och, stop yer worrying the day. The morrow wull take care o' itsel.'

Don't worry about things yet to come.

'Stumblin' helps ye richt yer fall.'

Stumbling can put you on your guard against falling.

'A wee keek back keeps ye oan the right path.'

Let life's experiences help you.

'Dinnae buy anythin' fae a man pantin' in the street.'

Don't buy from a doubtful source.

'Keep yer mind, heart an' hauns clean... then ye've nought tae worry aboot.'

If you have done nothing wrong then you have nothing to fear.

'They can see a midge a mile off but cannae see the wolf at their feet.'

Some folks are blind to problems close at hand.

'A rose also has a thorn.'

Do not take things for granted.

'He that blows in the stour fills his ain ee.'

If you stir up a problem some of the fallout may settle on you.

'Some compliments cost awfa dear.'

Watch, as some folks can pay dearly for flattery.

'Stamp oot the embers afore they become a fire.'

Address potential problems right away.

'Cast not oot the foul water till ye bring in the clean.'

Don't throw anything out until you have a suitable replacement.

'Slow doon oan lost paths.'

Don't be impatient if you really don't know where you are going in life.

'Ne'r trust muckle tae an auld enemy or a new freen.'

Be cautious in your dealings with old foes and people you have only recently become acquainted with.

'Dinnae trouble trouble till trouble troubles you.'

Don't go looking for problems.

'A hungry louse bites sair.'

Never underestimate anyone.

'Dinnae cut doon a tree that gies ye fruit an' shade.'

Be careful with the decisions you make.

'Ye cannae die twice, but pit aff the wance.'

Try and live as long as you possibly can.

'Appreciate what ye huv in case it becomes whit ye had.'

Look after what you already have in case you don't get any more.

'Dinnae break yer leg oan a step that isnae there.'

Be careful at all times.

'Some things urnae even worth a paper poke wi' a twirly end.'

Be careful as some things are just worthless.

'A raggit coat is armour against the robber.'

A low profile can be useful at times.

'Courtesy is cumbersome to them that ken it no'.

Mannerless people find manners a burden.

'Tak care in love or in court.'

Love and justice are sensitive issues. Handle with care.

'A wise man disnae hae his doctor in his will.'

Use a bit of common sense.

'Clothes dinnae mak a monk.'

You cannot always judge someone by looking at the outward appearance.

'Ye need tae dae whit ye huv tae dae, afore ye dae whit ye want tae dae.'

You need to get your priorities right.

'Shadows dinnae mak a noise.'

Be on your guard at all times.

'Watch those who speak well o' you but harbour malice in their soul.'

Learn to appraise people's true feelings towards you.

'Dinna burn doon the hoose tae get rid o' the smell.'

Only take actions that are appropriate.

'Don't pit gloves oan a cat or it'll no' catch the mice.'

Don't take action that stops progress.

'Some folks hae aw their ain back teeth.'

Some people can be quite shrewd.

'Better tae see a coo's tail than a bull's heid.'

Keep away from danger.

'Nane can play the fool sae weel as a wise man.'

Many people can appear simple but are anything but.

'Remember, bad bridges break.'

Don't just assume that everything is well.

'Yawning might be bad manners but at least it's an honest opinion.'

You can tell a lot from body language.

'Your time is your ain. Dinna let ithers spend it fur ye.'

Don't let other people waste your life.

'Yer frien's jeelie piece aye tastes better than yer ain.'

People are very rarely satisfied with what they have.

'How ye see yersel depends on the angle o' the mirror.'

How you consider yourself depends on what your priorities are.

'Watch oot! The deil's bairns hae aye their daddy's luck.'

Be on your guard. Tricksters are about.

'There's mony a barber wid shave a beardless man.'

Be careful. Watch out for rogues.

'A lie is up an' doon Scotland afore the truth has its boots on.'

Always keep to the truth.

'Dinnae let the same flame burn ye twice.'

Watch you don't repeat your mistakes.

'Wee stones, naw big hills, trip the unwary.'

Sometimes it's the less obvious problems that can give you heartache.

'Life is a wee bitty luck and a wee bitty judgement.'

Try to choose wisely.

'Jist hope butter sticks tae yer breid.'

We all need a bit of luck.

'The day hae eyes an' the nicht hae lugs.'

Don't give into temptation. Someone will always be aware of what you are doing.

'A rich man has mair cousins than his fether had kin.'

Money can attract rascals.

Health

'A sair back maks ye think.'

Sometimes you do not appreciate your health until you have a problem.

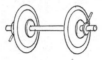

'Only clean oot yer ear wi yer elbow.'

Watch what you put in your ear.

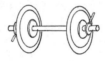

'Clean yer wallies twice a day an' they'll be with ye twice as lang.'

Look after your teeth.

'Ah'm fair puckled.'

I'm out of breath.

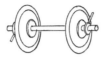

'He that eats but ane dish seldom needs the dochter.'

If you overeat you could give yourself problems.

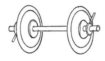

'Keep busy an' ye'll no' see auld Nick approaching.'

Concentrate on living.

'If yer the richest man in the Heilands an' yer health is poor... then so are you.'

Your health comes before everything else.

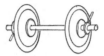

'A happy heart maks the face cheerful.'

If you are happy and content then your face will show it.

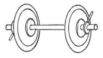

'A good walk cures the mind.'

Walking provides many benefits.

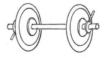

'Health is the wan treasure tae keep safe.'

Health is our real wealth.

'A red nose maks a ragged back.'

Excess drinking can impact both your standard of living and your health.

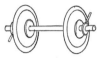

'Dree oot the inch as ye hae done the span.'

Get the most of your life, right up until the end.

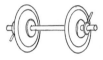

'Stick tae tell-worn paths an' keep oot o' the dark.'

Stay with what you know well.

'Wash yer hauns afore ye eat or ye willna be sure whit is goin' intae yer mooth.'

Personal hygiene is very important.

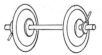

'Promises are like babes, fun tae make but difficult tae deliver.'

Keep your promises.

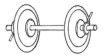

'We aw live in a wee hoose called yer body. So keep decorating it.'

Continually look after your health.

'Castor oil cures everything but a widden leg.'

Old cure for all health problems.

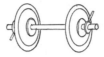

'An ounce o' prevention is worth a pun o' cure.'

Better to try to keep well rather than be ill and have to rely on medicines.

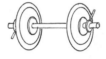

'Wash yer phizzog every day. That's whit a huv tae look at.'

Regardless of your situation, wash your face each day to brighten yourself up.

'May the cat eat you, an' the devil eat the cat.'

I wish you well.

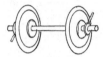

'A lang sleep an' a hearty laugh cures maist ills.'

The two fundamentals of health.

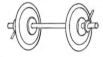

'Too much drink stops naithin' but a good sleep.'

Heavy drinking can cause disturbed sleep.

'A wabbit beggar is better than a sickly prince.'

Good health is important regardless of your position in life.

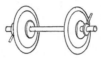

'Dinnae wear shoes that draw yer feet.'

Don't wear shoes that make your feet sweat.

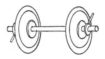

'Trim yer nails afore ye clean yer bum.'

Look after all aspects of your body.

'Health an' happiness are twin sisters.'

Both are interlocked to your overall wellbeing.

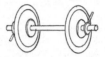

'Folks keep their doctor inside.'

Some people know instinctively what is good and bad for them.

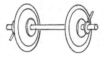

'Better six times wi' a sore heid than wan time deid.'

Stop complaining. You're fine.

International Tensions

'When bulls fight grass gets trampled.'

When nations fight it is always the ordinary folk who suffer.

'If you run wi' wolves you must howl wi' them.'

If you join the pack then you will need to adopt their ways.

'Revenge an' ambition are aye hungry.'

Revenge and ambition are never at peace.

'He needs a lang shanket spoon that sups kail wi' the deil.'

You must always be on your guard when dealing with potential enemies.

'Careful noo. Losin' the heid an' madness are brithers.'

Be very sure before you take action.

'Dinna worry. Thunder clouds dinna always bring rain.'

Do not always think the worst.

'It taks twa tae fecht.'

All arguments have two sides to them.

'Tough times come; tough times go. Aye, on an' on an' on it goes.'

Difficult periods are part of the world's cycle.

'Real revenge means ye dinna become like yer foe.'

Stick to your own standards.

'When the storm sweeps by, the wicked wull be gone.'

Those on the side of good will ultimately win.

'Och. Twelve herrings an' a bagpipe dinna mak a rebellion.'

Things are not as bad as they seem.'

'Arm yersel wi' the weapon o' common sense.'

Be sensible in all your actions.

'You've aye goat tae stand up fur whit's right even if ye staun alane.'

Be true to your principles.

'Watch yer neighbour's freens.'

You can tell what people are like by the company they keep.

'Ye cannae shake hauns wi' a maun whose fist is aye clenched.'

Some people are always aggressive.

'Watch. Some coos hae horns.'

Do not assume things.

'Countries must inhale courage an' exhale fear.'

Everyone must be resolute in times of a national emergency.

'The langest day wull hae an end.'

All things eventually come to an end.

Climate

'Aw trees breathe guid air.'

Trees produce the very oxygen we need.

'We have tae be awfa careful. Ye canny buy better weather, ye ken.'

World weather is vital to the planet.

'Ye've got tae keep the place tidy for the bairns.'

We must be mindful of the next generation.

'Neglect the croft, neglect the land.'

We all have to do our bit to look after Scotland.

'The heat o' the sun brings a wee bit o' health an' happiness tae the folks.'

Especially to a cold country like Scotland.

'Kill the Earth an' ye wadna hae onywhere else tae go.'

We need to look after our home planet.

'Protect the wee burdies or whistlin' wull stoap.'

We will regret it if we don't take care of nature.

'Recycling is aw right, but ah did it wance an' fell aff ma bike!'

Cheeky remark from a grandmother.

'Carbon footsteps might mak a right mess o' ma kitchen flair!'

Another cheeky remark by the same grandmother!

Family

'Be good, an if you cannae be good, be careful. An if you cannae be careful, name it efter me!'

Granny's tongue in cheek warning to her grandchildren.

'Newly laid eggs think they're smarter than the hen.'

The younger generation believe they know everything.

'Fruit frae the same branch can taste awfa different.'

Families come in all shapes and sizes.

'The stout horse aye gets the work.'

The willing member of the family always gets landed with most tasks.

'Dae weel an' dread nae shame.'

Do your best and you will have nothing to be ashamed of.

'Fools and bairns should no' see work half done.'

Be an example to your family.

'As the auld cock crows, the young cock grows.'

The young learn from the action of their elders.

'Between three an' thirteen thran the woodie when it's green.'

Train children early in life.

'Young folks cannae see a dyke in their road.'

Younger people don't always see the problems older folks see.'

'Naethin' is got withoot pains but an' ill name.'

Only bad reputations are achieved without effort.

'Fireside pleasure beats aw.'

You cannot do better than have family around you.

'Love has wan e'e an' is o'er deef.'

Love means you sometimes can ignore your loved one's faults.

Communicating

'The listening an' the hearing are different things.'

Concentrate on what someone is saying.

'That's pit yer gas at a peep.'

That's put you in your place.

'Prudent folks haud their tongue.'

In many instances it is better to remain silent.

'A nod's as guid as a wink tae a blind horse.'

Make your meaning clear.

'Hell slap it intae ye.'

It's your own fault.

'Mockin's catchin'.'

If you mock someone you mock yourself.

'Open yer lugs afore ye speak.'

Listen carefully to what is being said before you talk so you can properly address the subject.'

'Truth wull aye staun by itself.'

Integrity will stand up to scrutiny.

'Better tae hae sumbuddy else praise ye than hear it fae yer ain lips.'

Self praise is no praise.

'Awa an' bile yer heid.'

Don't talk rubbish.

'The big mooth o' a fool could bring ruin.'

Think before you speak.

'Haud yer wheesht.'

Please be quiet.

'Jist you tak care o' yer ain onions.'

Mind your own business!

'A kindly word can solve mony a big problem.'

Being gentle in your speech can resolve problems.

'Be canny wi' ithers' toes when yer mooth stomps aboot.'

Be careful what you say in company.

'Some folks believe aw whispers.'

People are inclined to believe anything that's whispered in their ear.

'Gonnae no' dae that.'

Don't do that.

'Don't pit baith feet in yer mooth at the same time or ye'll no' have a leg tae stand oan.'

Watch what you say.

'He that says whit he likes will hear whit he disnae like.'

If you're not diplomatic in the way you speak then you may hear unkind things about yourself.

'Yon's pure dead brilliant.'

It's just great.

'Three men can keep a secret if twa are deid.'

Best if you keep secrets to yourself.

'Back tae auld claes an' purridge.'

Returning to the normal pattern of life.

'Ye cannae shove yer granny aff a bus!'

Be thoughtful when it comes to the older generation.

Improving Yourself

'Turn yer wailin' intae dancin'.'

Be positive in life.

'Say it softly on yer pillow.'

Sleep on your problems.

'Be good an' dae the richt thing even when naebuddy is watchin'.'

Always be true to yourself and others.

'Look at the sun an' yer shadow wull be behind ye.'

Be positive.

'Life's a rainbow. Ye need sun an' rain tae gae it colour.'

You require a mixture of experiences to have an interesting life.

'Guid claes an' keys let ye in.'

Dressing as well as possible can help you in life.

'Beards dinna mean wisdom. Look at goats.'

You can't tell from appearances how clever a person is.

'Be whit ye seem an' seem whit ye are.'

Be true to the way you project yourself.

'He that gets first tae the hill can sit where they want.'

Being early has a significant advantage.

'A wise man can get learnin' fae them that has nane themselves.'

You can learn from everybody.

'Live as if ye wid die the morn.'

Have a good life with no regrets.

'Keep dirty boots oot yer heid.'

Only think positive thoughts.

'Experience teaches fools, an' maist fools wilna learn nae ither way.'

Foolish people only learn from their mistakes.

'Talking disnae mak purridge.'

Remain active.

'Calm waters gie nae skill tae tars.'

Easy tasks won't enhance your skills.

'Dinna wait till the iron is hot.'

Get ready for your opportunity and take it.

'O'er much rest causes rust.'

To have a good mind keep active.

'At least failin' means yer playin'.'

Even if you don't succeed it's important to have tried.

'In life sometimes ye win, other times ye learn.'

You can gain experience even when you lose.

'If ye get tae the door o' yer ambitions, kick that door aff it's hinges.'

There should be no limit to your ambitions.

'Better master ane than fight wi' ten.'

Better to be good at one thing than struggle with many.

'A sharp nose indicates yer nosy, an' a flat nose says ye wur too nosy.'

Don't be over inquisitive.

'Nae whip cuts sae sharp as the lash o' conscience.'

There is nothing worse than a guilty conscience.

'Idleness points the road tae nowhere.'

You will never get anywhere in life unless you work for it.

'Dinnae go an' smoke yer socks.'

Don't do anything crazy.

'Ye need tae dae whit ye have tae dae, afore ye can dae whit ye want tae dae.'

Make sure you plan out your life.

'Truth isnae invented; just lies.'

It is better to always tell the truth.

'Your last mistake's a rare teacher.'

Keep on learning from your mistakes.

'Old age disnae always bring wisdom.'

Keep up to date by thinking young.

'Some folks dinna need a granny; they are clever already!'

Many can achieve life's goals by themselves.

'Have a wee keek roon the corner. It might just be opportunity coming along.'

You never know what chances will happen.

'Committees aw plan crookit hooses.'

It's better to make your own plans.

'Learnin' folks can be gey old folks.'

By continually learning something new you can keep yourself active and alert.

'If yer road has a deid end, then change direction.'

Try all possible solutions.

'As guid may haud the stirrup as he that loups.'

Everyone is equal. Both the groom and the horse rider.

'Dinnae say ye cannae dae it till ye've tried ten times ten.'

Keep on going regardless.

'Some auld sparrows are ill tae tame.'

Changing someone set in their ways can be difficult.

'Aim fur the moon even if you only hit the lamppost outside yer granny's hoose.'

High ambition is to be admired.

'One day you will thank yersel for no' givin' up.'

Keep on trying!

'Aw buddy should hae a guid conceit o' themselves.'

Confidence is essential to self-improvement.

Love

'A person wi' a true frien disnae need a mirror.'

A good friend will keep you right.

'Tae the faithful show yerself faithful.'

Support those true to you.

'You twa should get merit. There's nae use spilin' twa hooses.'

Better to marry each other rather than get involved in an unsuitable match with someone else.

'Be a rock fur somebuddy or be friendly wi' somebuddy who can be yer rock.'

Everyone needs someone they can depend on.

'Love is a fearless giant.'

True love conquers all.

'Never marry a widow unless her first husband wis hanged.'

The good first husband of a widow is a difficult act to follow.

'Takers eat well an' givers sleep well.'

Kindly people tend to have an easy conscience.

'When petticoats woo breeks may come at speed.'

When the fair sex indicate interest usually males are interested.

'It is better tae marry o'er the midden than o'er the muir.'

It is usually better to marry someone in your own circle of interest.

'Love an' the cold catch on.'

Love can be infectious.

'Never gloat aboot somebuddy's ill fortune.'

Be supportive of people down on their luck.

'Pit yer arm roon the broken-hearted.'

They will need your support.

'Love overcomes the reasons o' the mind.'

The heart rules the head.

'Don't marry aff coos and cockerels.'

Some people are not a good match.

'It's gie easy tae halve the totty when there is love.'

You will happily share your lot with someone you love.

'Dinnae go over yer vineyard a second time or pick up grapes that huv fallen.'

If you have plenty be generous to others.

'Love is just as warm among cottars as courtiers.'

Love affects everyone.

Practical Actions

'If it's drownin' yer after, dinnae torment yersel wi' shallow water.'

If you wish to succeed put your whole self into the project.

'If yer scared o' wolves keep oot their den.'

Keep away from bad people.

'Dinnae remove the landmarks fae oor fathers.'

Keep up the standards established by generations gone by.

'Better late here than o'er early wi' the angels.'

Slow your pace down. Better ten minutes late in this world than ten years early for the next.

'There is little fur the rake efter the brush.'

Carry out tasks in a logical way.

'Cracked bells ne'r mend.'

Don't waste your time on tasks that are impossible.

'You wull just need tae swallow a coo.'

You will just need to accept that situation.

'Being willin' is guid but the doin' is better.'

Get on and do what you need to do.

'A dug wi' twa owners is twice hungry.'

Know who is responsible for each action.

'Skilled tars need nae luck wi the wind.'

Experience can overcome most situations.

'Dinnae dance oan a wee widden boat.'

Be sensible.

'A bald heid is soon shaven.'

Every situation has some advantage.

'Empty words dinnae fill an empty belly.'

You need to take action rather than just talk about it.

'Facts are chiels that winna ding.'

You cannot argue with reality.

'Excuses are gie poor patches oan the coat o' failure.'

Just do a good job in the first place.

'Ye dinnae have tae drink the sea.'

Don't exaggerate the situation.

'Awa an' go yer dinger.'

Go and get on with it.

Observations on Life

'Stay away fae the muck.'

You will become dust yourself soon enough.

'Life is o'er afore ye blink.'

So don't pass your time on worthless actions.

'Watch. Some folk's lying lips are never silent till the grave.'

Unfortunately, a few people continually exaggerate and lie.

'Ah must write that oan ma ear.'

I must try and remember that.

'Even lions get weak an' hungry.'

Everyone has their weaknesses.

'Batchelor's wives an' auld maid's bairns are aye well fed.'

Some people have no experience of certain aspects of life.

'Ye'll get a bit an' a bridle if ye cannae control yersell.'

Don't make me take extreme measures.

'Ah wid gnash ma teeth at ye but they're oot at the minute.'

I have a set of false teeth.

'Winking can get ye a black eye.'

Watch what you are about.

'The road tae a freen's hoose is ne'er lang.'

Anticipating something good keeps us going.

'Icy puddles dinnae recognise the toffs.'

Even important people have to be careful.

'The best way tae think... is fur yersel.'

Use your own judgement.

'Dinnae just blame the dug.'

It's easy to blame someone who can't argue back.

'May ye live it up for a hunner years, an' then get wan mair tae repent.'

Have a great life.

'The same boiling water that softens yer potato hardens yer egg.'

It's your choice how you act in life.

'If ye hae luck in the morn you'll hae luck in the evenin'.'

May you have continued good fortune.

'When God closes a door he opens a window.'

Something else will turn up.

'The older the fiddle the sweeter the tune.'

Experience can bring benefits.

'A used key disnae rust.'

Keep busy and educate yourself through life.

'Some folks are that clever they can hear a smell.'

Some people seem to have extra powers.

'Aw yin spies themselves first in photos.'

We are all self conscious.

'Aw life's purpose is doing.'

The purpose of life is life with a purpose.

'When sorrow sleeps, wake it not.'

Don't always be thinking sad thoughts.

'There's mair to ploughing than whistling.'

Some things are not as easy as you may think.

'Speak o' the deil an' he'll appear.'

If you talk about someone the chances are they will appear.

'Yon's no' even a ping oan a wee bowl.'

He is empty headed.

'Some wid marry a midden fur its muck.'

Some people will go to all lengths to obtain wealth.

'Ane at a time is guid fishin'.'

Be content with your life.

'It wis a sair fecht fur jist half a buttered scone.'

Sometimes you never fully achieve your goals.

'We're a' Jock Tamson's bairns.'

We are all equal.

'Too mony irons in the fire, and some maun cool.'

Don't take on numerous tasks at the one time or you may fail with some.

'Daylight wull keek through a sma' hole.'

There is no way of preventing some things.'

Wrinkles are painted wi' the brush o' experience.'

Age means you surely must have learned a lot.

'It's hangin' fae ma bottom lip shoutin' Tarzan!'

Find the article yourself.

'If aw men stuck tae their talents the coos wid be well milked.'

If everyone did what they were good at the world would be a better place.

'Life is too short tae drink whisky o'er watered.'

Life is brief so make the very best of it.

'Whit's fur ye wull no' go by ye.'

What is going to happen to you will happen.

'Dinnae expect somethin' new fae an echo.'

Let's be realistic.

'When it gets really dark you can see the stars.'

Even in difficult situations a solution may appear.

'Dinnae look back unless the view is good.'

Keep progressing with your life.

'A scabby sheep infects the flock.'

Watch who you mix with.

'Empty pockets shouldna stop you. But an empty heid wull.'

You need to have an idea how to resolve all problems.

'Dinna be feart tae try; only be feart no' tae try.'

Be positive in life and go for it.

'Anybody can be nice when the sun is oot shining. It's in a storm ye find oot wha' cares.'

True friends will assist regardless of how bad things get.

'They that finds keeps; they that loses seeks.'

Keep your possessions safe.

'It's naithin' but a gold ring oan a pig's nose.'

They may have money but they don't have class.

'Better tae bust oot than rust oot.'

Keep yourself busy.

'Don't be a lodging hoose cat.'

Don't just laze around doing nothing. Remain active and earn your keep.

'Life isnae fair but it can be guid.'

There are good and bad times in everyone's life.

'Yer eyes might hae fear but yer hauns are still at their work.'

You are being brave.

'Act daft an' get a free hurrel.'

Sometimes it may be better to let people assume you know nothing about a subject.

'The toon clock's stopped but at least it's right twice a day.'

Everything has its uses.

'Some cannae stop watchin' their work.'

They are lazy.

'Yer spirit is the lamp that shines oot o' ye.'

You are what is in you.

'The poor wi' courtesy are rich.'

Poor people with manners are gentry.

'Lang may yer lum reek, an' may a wee moose never leave yer kitchen press wi' a tear in its ee.'

May you live long and have sufficient food to eat.

'Yon's a right auld cock-a-doodle-do.'

They are forever crowing about something.

'Keep the heid an' kerry oan.'

Don't get angry but continue as normal.

'Yon's a right bampot.'

They are very silly.

'The day to come seems langer than the year that's gone.'

Waiting on an event can seem like ages.

'Ambition's a bonnie seed.'

Nothing can stop ambition growing.

'The crowd's appeal maks aw proud.'

Public affection makes one feel special.

'A common blot is nae stain.'

Don't worry about small faults that most people have.

'The wan's aye welcome that comes wi' a crookit oxter.'

Anyone bearing a gift is always welcome.

'The trade aye come half-an-oor late.'

Tradesmen are always late.

'Throwin' dirt digs yer ain hole.'

Belittling other people gets you nowhere.

'Honour an' envy dinnae haud hauns.'

They are incompatible.

'The dug is mair important than the collar.'

You are better to concede on unimportant issues than important ones.

'Mirrors gae ye whit ye want tae see.'

We usually only see what we want to.

'A pinch o' fear an' a' buddy's guid.'

The fear of punishment can deter the wrongdoer.

'Follow his path and know the man.'

You can only know someone by their deeds.

'Awa an' dry yer chin.'

Be quiet.

'A vaunter an' a liar are muckle aboot a' thing.'

People who exaggerate or lie are very similar.

'Langest at the fireside soonest finds cauld.'

Spoiled people can find it difficult to deal with life's downturns.

'A dog winna howl if ye hit him wi' a bane.'

Give someone what they want and they are unlikely to complain.

'Eagles flee alane, but sheep herd thegither.'

Some people can always accomplish tasks by themselves.

'Pointin' means wan finger oot an' three tae yersel.'

Sometimes we can be more at fault than those we blame.

'Fresh eyes at hame see aw things.'

Visitors appraise your home.

'A cat's a tiger in its ain hoose.'

You are the boss in your own home.

'They've goat the look o' wet clay aboot them.'

They look as though they are not long for this world.

Luath Press Limited

committed to publishing well written books worth reading

LUATH PRESS takes its name from Robert Burns, whose little collie Luath (*Gael.*, swift or nimble) tripped up Jean Armour at a wedding and gave him the chance to speak to the woman who was to be his wife and the abiding love of his life. Burns called one of the 'Twa Dogs' Luath after Cuchullin's hunting dog in Ossian's *Fingal*. Luath Press was established in 1981 in the heart of Burns country, and is now based a few steps up the road from Burns' first lodgings on Edinburgh's Royal Mile. Luath offers you distinctive writing with a hint of unexpected pleasures.

Most bookshops in the UK, the US, Canada, Australia, New Zealand and parts of Europe, either carry our books in stock or can order them for you. To order direct from us, please send a £sterling cheque, postal order, international money order or your credit card details (number, address of cardholder and expiry date) to us at the address below. Please add post and packing as follows: UK – £1.00 per delivery address; overseas surface mail – £2.50 per delivery address; overseas airmail – £3.50 for the first book to each delivery address, plus £1.00 for each additional book by airmail to the same address. If your order is a gift, we will happily enclose your card or message at no extra charge.

Luath Press Limited
543/2 Castlehill
The Royal Mile
Edinburgh EH1 2ND
Scotland
Telephone: 0131 225 4326 (24 hours)
Fax: 0131 225 4324
email: sales@luath.co.uk
Website: www.luath.co.uk